The Kid's Guide
Louie
The Labrador Retriever

Written by A.J. Richards
Illustrated by Rayah Jaymes

The Kid's Guide to Louie the Labrador Retriever

ISBN-13: 978-1502387462

Disclaimer: The information in this book does not replace a consultation with a veterinarian and/or a behavior consultant and may not be used to diagnose or treat any conditions in your dog. Dog training is not without risks. When in doubt, consult a professional dog trainer or canine behaviorist. AJ Richards cannot guarantee that your dog will instantly start to behave. Like anything in life, dog training requires work. Any issues that arise would depend on too many factors beyond our control, such as: The amount of time you are willing to invest in training your dog, your ability to apply what you have learned and the possibility that your dog may have a rare genetic or health condition affecting it's behavior. AJ Richards cannot guarantee any method will work for you and is not liable in any case of sickness, injury, or death.

Book Cover and Design by
Vermilion Chameleon Illustration and Design
www.vcartist.com

Printed in the USA

To my sister, Kadi,
who will always be a softy
for Labrador Retrievers.
A.J.

To my landlord,
please let me have a dog.
R.J.

This Book Belongs To:

_____

Your Name

_____

Your Dog's Name

Hello! My name is Louie.
I am a **Labrador Retriever.**
Would you like to hear my story?

I was born on the island of **Newfoundland**. Lots of people think that I was born in **Labrador** because of my name. Newfoundland and Labrador is one region of **Canada**.
Let me show you.

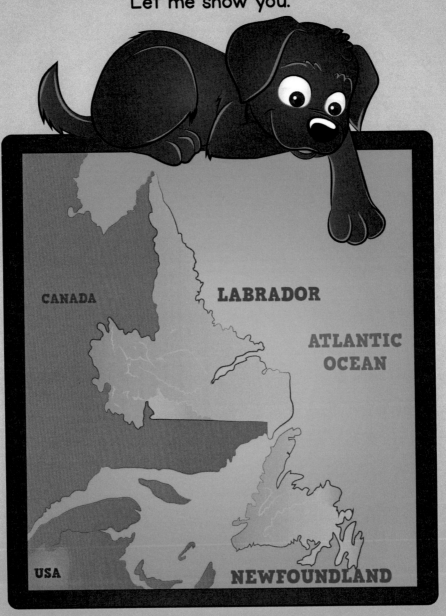

CANADA

LABRADOR

ATLANTIC OCEAN

USA

NEWFOUNDLAND

Where were you born? Can you find it on this map?
It is always okay to ask for help if you need it.

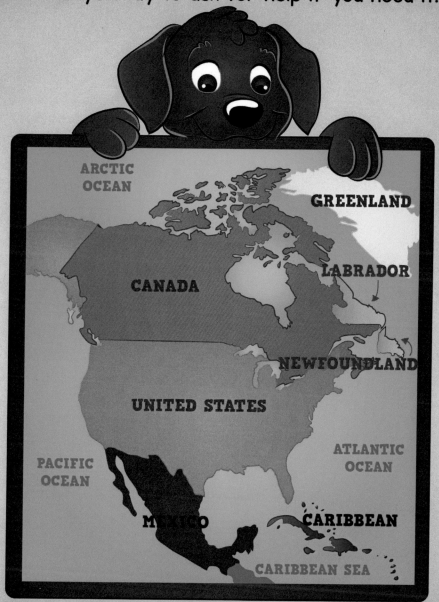

I have lots of family in Canada, but we moved to the
United States of America to work.

Where do you live?

Can you find it?

My Dad's job is so cool! He is a **guide dog**. A nice man needed his help. He helps people who can't see find their way around. Dad says, "When I am working, please do not pet me without **permission**." Guide dogs have to do a lot of training to be good at their job. They are very serious when they are working and cannot play. They also wear special vests with a handle to help guide their owners. It is a neat vest.

My Mom works with the police.
She says, "People hide stuff and it is my job to find it with my nose."
She has a very strong **sense of smell**.
Scientists say she can find
1 rotten apple in 2,000,000 **barrels**.
That is a lot of barrels!

How high can you count? I like to count, too! Ready?! Okay!

One time a day, I need to go for a walk or a run.

Two times a day, I should be **fed** when I am a grown up **dog**.

Three, four times a day, I should be fed as **puppy**.

Eight, nine, ten
ways I will teach you
how to take care of
me. Are you
ready to learn?

Five, six, seven
days are in a week.
Time to **brush my coat**.

My Mom says that I can come live with you if you make your home **safe** for me.

My Dad had to **puppy proof** our home before my brothers, sisters, and I could come home from the **veterinarian's** office. I think that means we needed to be watched all the time so we would not get into things that would hurt us.

You will need to puppy proof your home, too.
Pick things up off the floor so I don't make a mess or hurt myself.

I will tell you a secret. I like to chew things! Small things, big things, old things, and new things. Hot things, cold things, round things, and square things. Red things, blue things, spiky things, and smooth things.

Your whole family will need to work together to
feed,
groom,
and
exercise
me so I am **safe** and **healthy**.

I LOVE FOOD!

What food do you eat? I can only eat **natural** food or I will get sick. I circled the best food for us both to eat so we can grow up to be healthy and strong.

Fish

Fast Food

Carrots

Ice Cream

Brown Rice

Soda

18

Be careful!
Some food can be good for you, but not for me.
Please never feed me:

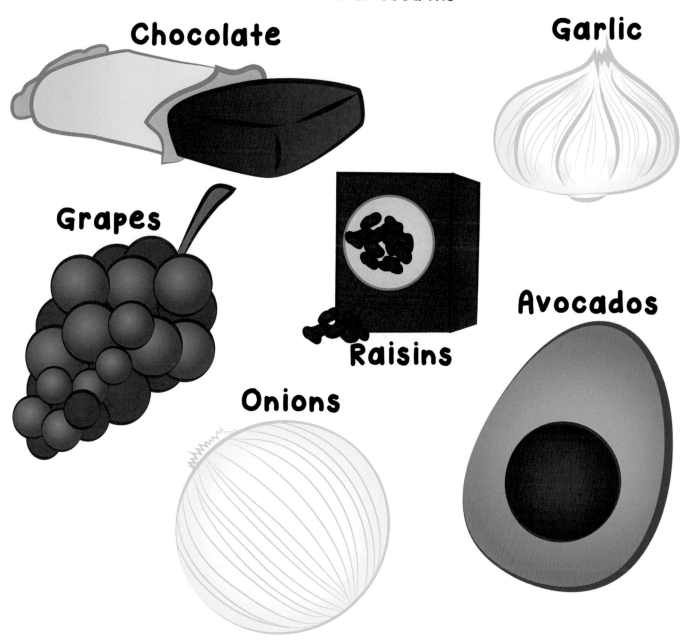

Chocolate

Garlic

Grapes

Raisins

Avocados

Onions

I know I may seem like a lot of work at first,
but best friends help each other.

My Dad once told me, "Louie, you will make a family very **happy**. Just treat them the way you want to be treated."
If you teach me, I will do whatever you like to do. You can train me to know the best ways to treat our family and friends so we are all happy. How do you like to be treated?

I have two **cousins** in Canada named, Buck and Ranger.
Buck is a yellow Labrador Retriever and Ranger is a chocolate
Labrador Retriever.
Buck always says, "People will not know what you do and what you
do NOT like unless you tell them."
Buck doesn't like people to **pet** his paws.

Ranger doesn't like people to pet his **muzzle**. Ranger always says,
"The best way to show people that you don't like something is to
just walk away."

My Dad told me **dog trainers** teach families the best ways to be kind and take better care of each other.
He says, "We all have to learn our **manners**."

Training takes practice.
I can't wait to get started.
I love to learn new things!

Ready?!
Okay!

When a **guest** is in our home, please ask an adult for help so we are not alone. I do NOT like to be **teased**, and please ask our guests not to move too fast. Please do not pull on my tail or poke me. Be careful! I might bite if I am **growling**, backing up, or showing my teeth.

Ask our guests to **squat** down, turn a little to the side, and pat their legs then wait until I come over to say, "Hi."

When I am ready to make friends,
I will **sniff** our **guests** and lean toward them.

The most important thing to me is that we are happy.
When I am happy, I **wag** my tail.
What do you do when you are happy?

Exercise makes me happy. We have to go for a walk every day.
My Mom told me my new family would teach me how
to go on walks wearing a **leash**.

She said, "Walking on a leash takes practice."
I should never pull you or walk in front of you. I may not like it at
first, but I will be much happier if you make me walk next to you.
My Mom is really smart.

I like to run and **fetch**. I love swimming too!
I also like to cuddle and I love to **play**.

I do not like to sit
around watching television
and playing video games
all day.

What do you like to do?
I hope you like to play too.

Sometimes I jump and knock people over even if they are not playing with me. Please help me be kind and learn how to **play** the right way.

When we **play,** we should not roll around on the ground together. I don't want you to get hurt. Stand up big and tall so I can look up to you.

29

Be **patient** with me when I am learning.
My Dad always said,
"Remember Louie, **practice makes perfect**."

Practice with an adult to learn the best ways to:

brush my coat

brush my teeth

give me baths

clean my ears

and

clip my nails

These grooming habits keep me healthy.

I will be patient with you too as we learn together.

Thank you for learning how to take care of me.
I think we are going to make each other very happy.

Love,
Louie

Resources

Glossary

Bath: Labs only need baths when they are dirty. Too many baths make their skin dry. (Ask an adult for help.)

Barrel: A large object made out of wood used to move or hold liquid. Holds up to 32 gallons.

Brush (my coat): Once a week use a brush from the pet store to keep the Lab's coat clean and the skin from getting dry.

Brush (my teeth): Use a soft toothbrush and toothpaste for dogs only. Lift the dog's lips and gently brush the teeth once a day. (Ask an adult for help.)

Canada: A country in northern North America, the second largest country in the world. About 33,000,000 (thirty- three million) people live there. The capital is Ottawa and the people speak English and French.

Clean (my ears): If your dog's ears look dirty or waxy, clean the parts of the ears you can see with a cotton ball or tissue. Use special soap from the vet or pet store. (Ask an adult for help.) If your dog is scratching or shaking his or her ears a lot or they are red and smell bad, take him or her to the vet. (Ask an adult for help.)

Clip (my nails): Long nails hurt and make it hard to walk. Cut them with clippers from the pet store or have the vet clip them when they get too long. (Ask an adult for help.)

Count: To add up to get the total number of something. (Count on: To depend on with full trust or confidence.)

Cousin: In a family, a child of one's uncle or aunt.

Feed: To give food.

Fetch: To go after something and bring it back.

Glossary

Dog: An animal (canine) with four legs that lives with people in their homes or has jobs to help people be safe.

Dog Trainer: A person who teaches dogs how to act around people and other animals.

Exercise: Moving the body so it will be healthy and strong.

Groom: To keep clean and healthy.

Growling: A low or harsh rumbling sound that comes from the throat of a dog when he or she is angry.

Guest: A person or animal invited to someone's home or activity.

Guide Dog: A dog trained to lead a blind person.

Happy: Feeling pleasure or joy because of your life or an event.

Healthy: Free from illness or injury.

Labrador Retriever (Labs): A medium to large shorthaired dog that is black, yellow, or chocolate in color. Labs are easy to train, smart, gentle, and family friendly.

Leash: A strap for leading an animal.

Manners: Nice ways of behaving towards others.

Muzzle: The nose, mouth, and chin area on the face.

Natural: Coming from the Earth. (Plants, trees, birds, fish)

Patient: Able to wait without getting angry.

Glossary

Puppy: A young dog.

Puppy proof: Making your home safe so your dog does not get sick or hurt. Learning what plants, medicine, cleaners, objects, and foods can make a puppy sick or hurt them, and keeping them locked away and out of reach. (Ask an adult for help.)

Rotten: Old food that is mushy or moldy.

Safe: Not going to be hurt or lost.

Scientists: A person who looks for the truth by testing guesses about the way things are in nature.

Sense of smell: Ability to know what is being smelled by using parts of the nose.

Sniff: Bring air into the nose to figure out what is being smelled.

Squat: To lower to the ground by bending the knees so the backs of the feet are almost touching a person's backside.

Teased: Making fun of or pretending to give someone something and then taking it away. Poking, pinching, or pulling a dog/puppy's tail, ears, or body.

Train: To teach a skill or behavior by giving directions and practicing it over a period of time.

United States of America: A country in North America that has 50 states and the District of Columbia with over 312,000,000 (three hundred and twelve million) people living there.

Veterinarian: A doctor who takes care of animals when they are hurt or sick.

Wag: When an animal's tail moves from side to side.

Feeding Chart
Labrador Retriever Puppy

As a rule of thumb puppies require:
Puppies should stay with the mother until 6 weeks (7 weeks is better)
Four meals a day from six weeks to three months (can be three if it works better with your schedule)

Three meals a day from three months to six months   **Two meals a day after that**

Puppy Weight in Pounds	Weaning to 3 Months	4 to 6 Months	7 to 12 Months	Over 12 Months
AMOUNT TO FEED IN CUPS PER DAY				
3 to 5	1/2 to 3/4	3/4 to 1		
5 to 10	3/4 to 1 1/2	1 to 2		
10 to 20	1 1/2 to 2 1/2	2 to 3	1 1/2 to 2 1/2	
20 to 30	3 1/2 to 5	2 1/2 to 3 1/2	2 to 2 1/2	
30 to 40		3 1/2 to 4 1/2	2 1/4 to 2 1/2	
40 to 60		4 1/2 to 5 1/2	3 1/4 to 4 1/4	2 1/2 to 3 1/4
60 to 80		5 1/2 to 6 1/2	4 1/4 to 5	3 1/4 to 4
80 to 100			4 1/2 to 5 1/2	4 to 4 1/2
100 to 120			5 1/2 to 6 1/2	4 1/2 to 5 1/2
120 to 140			6 to 6 1/2	5 1/2 to 6 1/4
140 to 160			6 1/2 to 7 1/2	6 1/4 to 6 3/4
160 to 180				6 3/4 to 7 1/2

The chart is only a guideline

When switching to adult dog food, do it slowly over the course of one to two weeks by gradually mixing in increasing amounts of the adult food with decreasing amounts of puppy food to minimize stomach upset.

Less Exercise = Less Food

If he/she gets too fat, cut back. If he/she gets too slim, add a bit more.

Educational Sites

American Kennel Club
http://www.akc.org/breeds/labrador_retriever/index.cfm

The Labrador Site
http://www.thelabradorsite.com/how-to-feed-a-labrador/
http://www.thelabradorsite.com/how-to-play-safely-with-a-labrador/

Public Broadcasting Service
http://www.pbs.org/wgbh/nova/nature/dogs-sense-of-smell.html

PetCareRX
http://www.petcarerx.com/article/how-to-make-home-made-dog-food-for-labradors/231

Parent's Magazine
http://www.parents.com/parenting/pets/kids/involve-kids-in-dog-training/

Vet Street
http://www.vetstreet.com/our-pet-experts/when-will-my-labrador-stop-chewing-on-everything

http://www.vetstreet.com/our-pet-experts/how-to-pet-a-dog

Pet Health 101 for Dogs & Cats
http://www.pethealth101.com/

Author

A.J. Richards, from an early age, has been surrounded by animals: dogs, cats, horses, deer, hamsters, gerbils, and many others to name a few. Also, caring for numerous shelter pets throughout her adulthood. She earned her Bachelor's degree in American Literature and a Master's in Public Administration while working with at-risk youth for a Nebraska non-profit. She now lives in Berkeley, California.

Illustrator

Rayah Jaymes is an illustrator, chef and musician that comes from an incredibly large multicultral family which continues to inspire her art and story telling.
She aspires to illustrate many more books that educate children and their parents about the diverse world around them and how they can make it better everyday in everything they do.

Find her and more of her books at www.vcartist.com

www.dogbooksforkids.com

More Books from A Puppy's New Home

Coming Soon

72104778R00024

Made in the USA
Middletown, DE
03 May 2018